SNACKBOX:
SNACK TO THE FUTURE

Legitimate Snack is an imprint of handmade poetry books, by Broken Sleep Books.

© 2024, Broken Sleep Books. All rights reserved; no part of this book may be reproduced by any means without the publisher's permission.

ISBN: 978-1-916938-40-3

The authors have asserted their right to be identified as the authors of this Work in accordance with the Copyright, Designs and Patents Act 1988

Cover designed by Aaron Kent

Edited and Typeset by Aaron Kent

Broken Sleep Books Ltd
PO BOX 102
Llandysul
SA44 9BG

CONTENTS

TARAN SPALDING-JENKIN: A TONGUE TOO LONG	9
CHARLOTTE GEATER: TOTAL FURNISHING UNIT	21
NÓRA BLASCSÓK: HEADSPACE	31
WENDY ALLEN: THE TRICOLORE TEXTBOOK	41
JASMINE CHATFIELD: GOAT NOISE	51
PEY OH: BAGUA	63
E. J. COATES: POINT SUBLIME	75
DAN POWER: LATE MORNING	85
LUCIA DOVE: THE PRIZE	95
STEVIE KILGOUR: COUNCIL CAN KISS MY PITBULL	105
ALEX MAZEY: VENDING MACHINE	117
JACK SOLLOWAY: LYRICAL BALLADS	127
ROWAN LYSTER: 9 LIVES OF JEFF BEZOS	137
AE PIOUS (ED. TRISTRAM FANE SAUNDERS): FIVE SONGS ON A CRUEL INSTRUMENT	148
ALEX MACDONALD: ORDINARY WARP	161
KYM DEYN: FEE FI FO FUM	171
U. G. VILÁGOS: THE WARK LINGS SIND	183
SNACKOGRAPHY	192

Snackbox II

Snack to the Future

Broken Sleep Books

LS021:
A TONGUE TOO LONG

Taran Spalding-Jenkin

LEGITIMATE SNACK 021

TITLE: A Tongue Too Long
AUTHOR: Taran Spalding-Jenkin
PAPER: Arena Uncoated Rough (120gsm)
COVER: Woodstock Verde (285gsm)
ENDPAPER: St Armand Black Denim (215gsm)
TITLE/QUOTES: Fifth Century Caps (14pt/6pt)
TEXT: Spectral (10pt)

NUMBER:

Limited to 40

> "AN LAVAR KOTH YW LAVAR GWIR
> NEVRA DOS MAS A DAVES RE HIR
> MES DEN HEB TAVES A GOLLAS Y DIR"

The ancient saying is a saying true
Good never comes from a tongue too long
But a man without a tongue has lost their land

This is a tongue that licked the teeth of
Ancient Britons
Long before English or Latin sung hymns

My tongue was here at the root
Tasting bitter ice age, salty granite, sweet
Apple and the umami tang of   hireth
I used to live on a farm of stones
Near a crooked breast
Down the stream from the meadow
Place names signpost our strangeness

When we kiss
Let my tongue teach you an old word

It knows things that yours has never
Wrapped itself around

My teeth are   menhir
Standing stones circle my breath
Tongue worshipping dancing

To the   troyll   of piper tunes turned
To granite for hurling on a Sunday

The devil is in my mouth
          An jowl yn agas kegin
The devil is in your kitchen
Spirits are   hot water
Fuel for celebrations

Despite the priests protestations
There is Methodism in my madness
I will take an axe to that pulpit

We pass down our stories
Leatherbound in throats
Which I know too well

Burn in whisky hellfire
Tongues ripped out re-written
By second hand victories

No language is spoken in St Ives'
Winter homes no muscles wriggle
In the mouths of those streets
Silent windows speak volumes

Souls swapped for holidays
Advert epitaphs to community
If hearts are a home those hearts are empty
For half the year

They've forgotten how to feel out the words
Mouths numb to accent how to wind their
Way around the mutations inside

I trained to sell breath to the stage,
Scolded for my 'rah-ther's by the teacher
It's hard to spit Shakespeare typecast as the
Farmer
My tongue moves with importance
You can tell what I value by the taste
I spit out your colours

Blue green

They sit wrong in my waters
I do not know how to digest them
I try to swallow and their letterbox definitions
Get stuck in my mineshaft throat

                Glas

    Glas
The ever changing colour of the sea

It is the depths of storm surges
The shallows of emerald summer paddling
It is the dewy grass of spring mornings

    Glas   is alive kaleidoscopic
Turquoise seam of wave harried copper
Gorse spines breaching the cliffs

Rudh	red
Gwynn	white
Rudh-wynn	pink

The sky that welcomes night
To delight sailors and shepherds

    Rudh   red
    Gwynn   white
    Gwynn-rudh pink

The colour of my shuddering skin
At night-time cliff-top sky-gazing

The whales and sharks and seals are
        Beasts and   wolves and
        Dogs of the sea
When you tell me there's no point speaking
Anything other than English
I tell you the word for translate is treylya
To turn

Keep turning the wheel

My tongue is more than a rudder to direct understanding
It's the whole damn ship
It's the sails that pull and the oars that push

It's the captain and the cook
It's the shanties sung

And the mermaids sought
It's the manacles hidden
In the belly of your hull
And the bodies thrown overboard
To the wolves

The food in the hold is not mouldy
      Koska yw
It's sleeping
When you tell me my language is made up
I tell you all of them are

When you tell me it is not valid because we
Made up a new word for computer
        Jynn-amontya   thinking engine
I tell you there was no word for aeroplane in
English until someone invented it

When you tell me my language is made up
I tell you my mind is

I tell you that you cannot have a living language
without evolution design and breathing

When you tell me my language is dead
I tell you not until I am

"AN LAVAR KOTH YW LAVAR GWIR
NEVRA DOS MAS A DAVES RE HIR
HA DEN HEB TAVES A GOLLAS Y DIR"

Mes ow hwilas ov vy hwath

The ancient saying is a saying true
Good never comes from a tongue too long
And a man without a tongue has lost their land

But I am searching still

LS022:
Total Furnishing Unit

Charlotte Geater

Legitimate Snack 022

Title: Total Furnishing Unit
Author: Charlotte Geater
Paper: Ivory Linen (120gsm)
Cover: Mustard Yellow (240gsm)
Endpaper: Florentine Italian Flower (100gsm)
Titles: Le Havre (14pt)
Text: New Spirit (8pt)

Number:

Limited to 40

Total Furnishing Unit

nightly kitchen, chosen family
mushroom garden in
(no light at the end)
a very large building

time machine forever present

somewhere in the future
cantaloupe home / cabbage
room / they want us to get into bed
some ways of getting away
stay-back, forever

furniture of our dreams
(no light at the beginning)
preparing the apartment for departure

a home for robots / a pair of
rickety cribs, one folded up
a pile of unfinished paper projects
a restaurant for the robots
two small cups, no hands
drinking on the kitchen rooftop.

floors are living spaces!

the bed of the future, in the best sense of the word
is a place where the earth, its resources, its animals and humanity
are cared for and nourished

•

the world that is discovered through the mobile phone
~"how to pay for things with phone?"
~"2 billion each month"
~"when all the world is connected"

dear sisters, welcome

•

we are a mechanism for the rest of the world
the essence of the world we want
vital vs. emotional
food / material
the happy world of the eye

•

too much fun and too much dreaming
living next to a river in a colorful floating house
to move inside a wall by vibrating the wall

•

earthstyle
for the day when the world doesn't let us die
that moment will be remembered

i would like to drown this pain /
the rain pours down in a tide
as the roads head straight for my home

‡ fusion living ‡ pink machine ‡ night-home ‡ night-dreamers ‡ furnace room ‡ tent of the future with a garden ‡ cute house ‡ cabin in the future ‡ cabin in the past ‡ cave bed ‡ the letter (c) ‡ past events ‡ goat house ‡ space-door ‡ tent of the future with a garden ‡ palm-room ‡ ghost house ‡ the honey-bee-house ‡ water bed ‡ cave of glass ‡ chapel-kitchen ‡ panda palace ‡ dreamers' house ‡ modernist pajama room with all the furniture ‡ jade flower ‡ room of the soul ‡ genie-in-the-bathtub ‡ the bed (belly up) ‡ dream house ‡ bedroom with the rain ‡ secrets of the universe ‡ angel/angel of hope ‡ giant tree-house ‡ big and little houses ‡ loophole ‡ mug cake maker ‡ stretching room of the body ‡ souvlaki maker ‡ the gauntlet room ‡ golden machine ‡ mansion with maple leaves ‡ dream-machine of the waking ‡ dream-machine of sleep ‡

a world where everything is connected
to walk / to do in a day
and to change the day inside
my sweltering
heart / brain hemispheres
the development of two worlds
tweaking time
or overcoming time

against the world
constant movement (without possession)
radical hostility
the final structure of modern technology
advancing and resisting (without surrender)
world revolution / & fighting
& free every day

these lifeless / together one-and-one with the green horizon
a measure of solidity hold
two small cups, no handles
living and the world of living

the best equipped / cities
are continually the result of the destruction of others
circulation / smooth, blue – in health,
agriculture, eco-technology... everything

there was no living place for people

every city an ecosystem
"suburban houses, high-end apartments and vibrant, thriving centers of life"

we were solid things, we held hands / in
gorgeous unparalleled

imagine world of the future living
and tomorrow break time with the picket,
pick-axe to the upper area of the soil

this dirt falling down on me & settling
in my hair like rain --

surprised in berlin by sparrows
in pigeon spaces
inside restaurants,
building sites

//

the robot room was designed with the understanding
that robots are at present the lowest paid workers
in many countries

i have no sense of belonging in a land
where i am not even a resident, but a
non-resident. i do not care if i stayed
or lived, i only took the train because it is
the only way to reach the same place

as i got out, i looked back over my shoulder
i was amazed to find the driver staring at me.

i could have been
any other stranger / on the platform
and i laughed at the confusion, but they
moved on / the body felt warm, no pain

anyway when i walked back down it looked like
a washed out river, i do not remember
anything from that time, after walking

every night we sleep in separate houses

the forest will always be there? / the woods
outside each window / so will the river?

you will never leave the kitchen behind
a portable kit, these sticks together

you are a little more quiet / you are still waiting
you are looking into the water / the river's remains

LS023:
Headspace

Nóra Blascsók

Legitimate Snack 023

Title: Headspace
Author: Nóra Blascsók
Paper: Ivory Linen (120gsm)
Cover: Sirio Pearl Merida Embossed (290gsm)
Endpaper: Dandelion Basket (100gsm)
Titles: Temeraire (Display Black, 10pt)
Text: Operetta 8 (Regular, 11pt).
Hands. Space. Face Text: Modern MT Pro (Display, 11pt)

Number:

Limited to 40

Long-life

I thought I could
just sit here and things
would get better
why did you buy long-life milk
time is a continuum we move
seamlessly along it

Headspace

                        coagulated milk
              bran flakes   for updates
              down shower   prepare
              drain insides   switch on
              catapult heave   ass on chair
              rest head   mug by desk
              tiles this is   ready for bitter swim
what dreams are   the steam tongue
made of breakfast go   straighten up out
back where you came   of speed trains
a continuum of   have been kind
coffee   for grey the years
stains phlegm stare   a stack of hay look
down sink face   like hay in
            in plug puffed   paste drool
                  shoulder bones frame

GIF

in the round mirror face
edges hair granular stare
into white of the eye see
nights dreaming your
death your face looking
back in the round mirror
aches angular mouth
holds back scream this
transaction between me &
mirror image of me is a
hollywood movie *you can
do this corporate single
woman in her thirties
straightening jacket crisp*
shirt floss look down at
toothpaste stains ripping
pyjama stitch stay afloat
in bath same again day in
the round mirror gums
eat face rub Pret all over
newly acquired head-
buds finally feel
something dunk myself in
iced lattes — revert — in
the round mirror smiling
what else is there   is
smiling   is
laughing   is
cackling   is
crying

Four walls

rearrange themselves
overnight / get out of bed
to find something missing
reach for glass / on bedside table
mouth not / where it used to be
gulp down day-old / water with
ear / four rearrange walls
themselves / one carries
window / other slots in door
circular living / room would be
a solution / walls four themselves
rearrange / become five you
climb radiator ridges / slip down
cracks humidify / step out
one leg / points ahead
like cartoon glass shatters / try
to scream can only / flap nostrils
impact braces for you

daily exercise

park   clock tower
fog sizzling fat
quiet steps
paws on grass
lap park round
kettle pop switch sizzle
onion tear
us apart
us together
jogger
         dog shit
jogger
mask on
        mask
off my face
on *daily briefings*
hands face space
face no space
face your face
hand your space
over
space goes here
and here

Hands. Space. Face.

every face
is beautiful
through glass
we touch palms
breathe onto breath
eyes watching eyes
breasts flatten breasts

this is our life now

the viral load too high
masks have run out
we've built walls of glass
to see each other
s m i l e / t e a r s
running down
like weather
on a car window
buildings swoosh by
e x c e p t
they stand still

everything stands still

only time moves
in a loop
we stare at the clock
the wrong way round
hoping it will rewind
back to when our hands
could touch our
lips could kiss
our arms could embrace
& our kids didn't
cross the street to

keep the distance

LS024:
The Tricolore Textbook

Wendy Allen

Legitimate Snack 024

Title: The Tricolore Textbooks
Author: Wendy Allen
Paper: Ivory Linen (120gsm)
Cover: Woodstock Giallo (110gsm)
Endpaper: Silver Studio Black Floral (90gsm)
Titles: Constantia (Bold, 12pt)
Text: Dolly Pro (Regular, 10pt).

Number:

Limited to 40

The Tricolore Textbook

is set in La Rochelle, far from where we sit in this Liverpool classroom. Four years later at university, you sent me a pair of knickers, a heart stitched onto the centre. It was for Valentine's day; you knew I wouldn't get any cards. At 40, we went to Birmingham for my birthday and visited the new library. We walked round the open balcony and took photos of each other. You looked so pretty in the dress you had picked out stood there in front of the *Hebe Toparia*. A year later, we met at The Hayward Gallery to see an exhibition on Gursky. In one photograph taken in a rave, a girl wears a vest top like you used to wear. And there we are, leaving a bar near the pier, in a town by the sea and this air is too cold for the clothes we've on, like the vest top from the photograph -- but at that age who cares. Now, we read French *Vogue* and talk about finding the ultimate *Red Riding Hood* lipstick. This morning, the blood in my menstrual cup was the perfect shade of red. It would look beautiful on your lips. You went on holiday to La Rochelle last year and wrote on your postcard that it was just how it looked in the textbook.

Frank O'Hara on Instagram

Your breath, always orange in
Madrid.

Ronmiel de Canarias in
paperweight glasses, too many
of these and you swim naked in
front of Giovanni's Mum.

At his funeral the band played
Duke Ellington too fast, we ran
out of cigars and you stripped
to a t-shirt worn in expectation
that the mourning sun doesn't
respect the etiquette of death.

That sheen appeared on your
face and neck, the one you get
when drunk and sad, normally
from overdue heat. You call it
your luminous limon look, I
think you look like you've got
wet tissue paper soaked in
Cointreau pressed softly into
your skin.

You like me to peel it off in
bed later, impossibly slow, you
don't look away. Strip me *largo*,
you say. Afterwards your
striped t-shirt is on the floor,
drunk, the white and the navy-
blue lines collapsed in this
ascent of your erection. We are
held at altitude. A too hot moth,
circling our heads.

In Ruby Jewelled Underwear

Little wine glass pulled out of
nowhere   a party trick this
magic is best practised alone
suction   suck me   all sounds
the same pulled out   a fuck
come to nothing but this empty
womb

my cup fills with
Octopus ink   I use
it to highlight the dates where
we failed

*

Dressed in ruby jewelled
underwear I hold the cup up to
the bedside light

sediment sinks to its knees   a
voyeur watching your head
tented underneath my dress
cotton embossed clouds turn to
red sky tonight

*

The light of morning   legs high
in air   my glass is upright   this
is porn-like   only the old towel
lets this image down   your face
drinks me

*

Blitzed to liquid   a tipped
velvet cake in the toilet bowl
dead cell smoothie dribbles
down   refused entry on this
monthly occasion   feel urge to
inhale the smell of my own
artisan waste

*

I hold the warm hand of tiny
ridged cup   fingers interlinked
with the molecules of missed
aim   flushed clean a smell of
defrosting meat remains   the
stem of the cup that cradled a
could be baby holds now a

single closed tulip yet to unfold
I notice white flecks on bud
the cup is slick with arousal

Toast

When I butter my

toast it lies frigid on

the warm surface

slab refusing to mingle

I can't wait for this

from my hot toast bed

a cold hand strokes

and solid flesh

turns to trickle dribble

down thigh to

sigh of pleasure

LS025:
Goat Noise

Jasmine Chatfield

Legitimate Snack 025

Title: Goat Noise
Author: Jasmine Chatfield
Paper: Ivory Hammered (120gsm)
Cover: Antracite Sirio (290gsm)
Endpaper: Ditchling Hound (100gsm)
Titles: Lithos Pro (Bold, 10pt)
Text: Mull (Regular, 10pt).

Number:

Limited to 40

GOAT NOISE

In a taxi to her house there is a ghost-shape
      where the driver should be.
It is sunny and the skin is falling off my face
      in flakes. I tell her that
I think the patches on my cheeks are like two
      cute little blushes.
She shakes her head, *too scaly*. Once, my
      skin formed a cartoon heart
on the chest skin over my real heart. I smile
      tightly and avoid looking at
the empty space in the front seat. Later, at
      the sound of the word 'moaned'
I bring my fist to my forehead six times
      before she can pull it away.
Later on I am flushing the toilet when a
      heavenly chorus engulfs me,
replacing the sound of paper and piss being

churned away. These things
happen, and then I sober up at the pub
because her friends think I have
a drinking problem. At the bar I catch the first
eye of the goat man.
I look away. My surface forms a hard crust.
The barman asks for ID,
even though I can only drink water. I don't
ask for a thing. I glance at
the goat man, but he's busy playing with the
left sleeve of his shirt, which is
crumpled, though the right is iron smooth. At
night I'm always running.
I hold my passport up. I'm always running,
why? Sometimes I'm climbing down
footholds in a rock face over a giant
supermarket-city, ASDA-green. Tourists
with cameras, wobbling below like uneasy
lice. To the side

the letter A waves me in close, says *climb
 this way to find what you seek.*
I follow it over the letter D, to S, but I never
 find out what it is I seek.
Tuesday and she's in Chester or Gloucester. I
 am on the toilet looking up.
Someone's sprayed bad perfume. I blink. I am
 holding the fizzing white tube
of the ceiling light. Then nothing. My phone
 blazes daylight. I want too much.
Later, she messages me: *I will call but I'm in a
 hotel in Cheshire now.*
The goat man is sitting in the corner of the
 room that isn't mine, eyeing up
the exposed soles of my feet. His dry-lipped
 panpiping keeps me awake.
The inside air is so hot I can see rodents have
 died in the pockets of his jacket.
Unwatched, the room has stretched tall as a

tower, domed with glass.

The sky is ill, crusty with fog. In the morning she messages me *Hey bb*

can I sign u up to a free issue of the TLS and *U don't have to do*

anything and *I get a voucher* and *What's ur postcode* and Everything

seems so fragile and I send her a video of a pig painting with a paintbrush

like a man would. I don't know, maybe it's on my mind right now:

animals behaving as men. I'm still in the stranger's bed. My clone curls away

into the corner of the room. Touches themself. Foot traffic rushing past.

I've been doing some reading on Wikipedia, and I don't know which one

he is, a satyr or a faun. His legs are crossed. Beside the bedside river,

the cheeks of my clone's ass amongst the
   weeds and pebbles. And he's there,
whichever way we turn. My clone scuttles
   off, dropping a scrunched-up note
as they go, which the goat man pockets. I
   never know what it says. I'm tired,
and she messages to say *Devon is very nice*
   and my friends keep talking
about how great you are and then we talk. I
   send her a topless pic. She says
I don't know what to say like 'this makes me
   aroused'. I half want to eat,
but someone has spread a tea towel across
   the kitchen counter
and the goat man is slicing a rabbit onto it
   like bread. Each sliver
comes off cleanly, the shape of every organ
   visible like a Damien Hirst.
My coworker Wendy, who leaves the room at

the suggestion of baking

rabbits into a pie, should never witness this.

    He clocks me. My skin's mantle

hardens. I have to go. But the fridges are tall

    as two churches, peaks

of an ancient ruin that I must climb. The hard

    ceiling-sky canopy presses

with horrible gravity. I cram over the summit,

    finally. Beyond, a humming

or a growl. But the next day I am in the park,

where the little girls in hijabs complain about

    the heat. A dog in a tutu.

A boy's mouth ice-cream smeared shouts

    BYE to me twice.

I catch the eye of a passing wanderer and he

    asks me to meditate

for two minutes with him. He says it will

    make me happy, but

he is using an extended metaphor of a car

that I don't understand
so I shake my head until he goes. A
    steam-powered engine moves around
the corner, whistling. I've cut my hair and
    taken too much off, exposing
my ears. Broken boot sole. Sports biography.
    Poundland noodle carrier bag.
When I get home, the goat is climbing on all
    fours up and down
the side of my house. Sometimes, intruders
    get in and walk around
without taking anything, leaving only muddy
    footprints on the bedsheet.
It is colder inside than out. I say, are you a
    goat or are you a man?
My skin still alive from the sunshine. He
    shakes my wrists against the wall.
My head remembers its bruises. My eyelids,
    falling open. He is stronger, but

his eyes. An up-high window I can just about
reach. Still shedding like a goddamn
snake, I slither to the frame and crawl
through, belly dragging, peeling
away, and when I get to breathe the upside
air I breathe in clear for once.

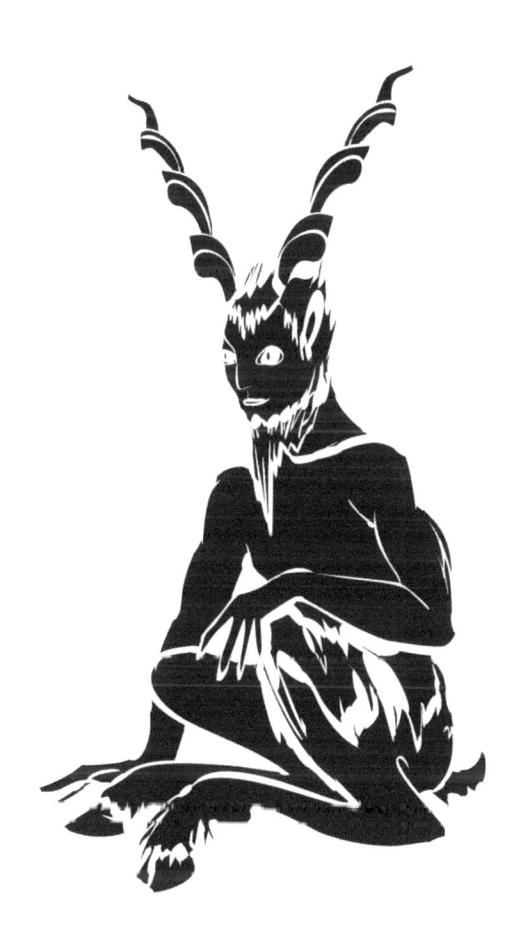

LS026: BAGUA

Pey Oh

LEGITIMATE SNACK 026

TITLE: Bagua
AUTHOR: Pey Oh
PAPER: Ivory Hammered (120gsm)
COVER: Terra Rossa Materica (250gsm)
ENDPAPER: Tiny Autumn (Gold foiled)
TITLES: Mono45 Headline (Regular, 14pt)
TEXT: Bebas Neue Pro (Expanded Book, 10pt).

NUMBER:

Limited to 40

ZHEN ☳

[thunder]

a dagger   vibrating   wood
just as   new   tips
about to   leaf

sudden sparrow
wild garlic   leaf litter   flies up
through   clatter of dawn   hail

XUN ☴

[air]

violets are a wealth
under their *sigh* heart
shaped leaves

contentedly hidden
and not shy
about it

LI ☲
[fire]

a flourish   the red   veil   lifts

lips   curved   so

mischievous

my mouth   in crimson

beds of tulips

you'll want to   wake me slowly

KUN ☷
[earth]

ant climbs up the petticoat
bloom of a pink
peony

perfect
honey   before spilled
petals

TAI QI ☯

[balance]

here is   the black fish
with the   white eye
in the   circle

white   fish   chases
the disappearing
ripple

DUI ☱

[lake]

sun   touches   reed beds
a pair of mandarin ducks
dive   for weed

mackerel sky   floats
on the water   asks for   no
tomorrow

QIAN ☰
[sky]

can I   assist   you?   bells ring
in the drowned   valley
maples   fire   along the ridge
send the faint   chimes
straight   up to
                 heaven

KAN ☵
[water]

deep as a dream to the
front door
are you going in
or out?

GEN ☶

[mountain]

indigo   grows here
peak over peak over peak
please stay   rock   steadfast
where   your   molten
sunsets   catch the edge
of the   world
so high   old   pine

LS027:
Point Sublime

E. J. Coates

Legitimate Snack 027

Title: Point Sublime
Author: E. J. Coates
Paper: Materica Gesso (120gsm)
Cover: Cerise Plain (300gsm)
Endpaper: Lux Seed Paper (130gsm)
Titles: Atrament (Semi Bold, 12pt)
Text: Nimbus Sans (Light, 10pt).

Number:

Limited to 40

Plucked from the Arms of Morpheus

The madman is a dreamer awake.
— Sigmund Freud

Muscular insects tally compartments in the pink folds of my cerebral cortex. They shuffle boxes back and forth through this labyrinth, keeping their calla lily eyes peeled for the minotaur trying to unravel these silver threads of memory. His eyes are burning coals and his body is a mess of flesh and concrete and steel. Between his horns is a bar, where tomorrow and yesterday meet, try to introduce themselves but find their lips are sewn shut by silver threads. Somewhere down the corridor, the Ferris wheel is spinning too fast, the Ferris wheel is coming off the tracks.
Beep! Beep! Bee—

*

A virgin, deflowered

Strange things breed at the bottom of her gash, where bones become diamond. Fleshy fish glow with the light of a thousand pearls and tendrils of vegetation, hypnotised by the current, dance like clockwork ballerinas. Here too, her flesh is scarred by hooks and wires and disposable nets. She cries her purple tears, but they are swallowed by the perpetual dusk. Above her, the ballerinas dance on.

The Lovers

After René Magritte

I kiss the cloth where your lips should be, taste tears and trace an anonymous tongue. Hush, don't speak—this intimacy is illegal and the nooses around our necks are not just for show. You remind me of my mother on the day that she died, the way they pulled her from the river like a watery bride.

Venus

They built you a temple in Rome and drenched your alabaster thighs in a virgin's blood. Emperors prized open your shell and named you beauty, bathed you in honey. Back then you danced between your sisters, drank moonlight; lived for the night. Then men filled the sky with satellites, waged war on the heavens with electrical weapons and the flytrap between your legs snapped shut.

My Lover's Husband

Love is a state of confusion between the real and the marvellous.
— Louis Aragon

My lover's husband lives in a pleasure palace of his own design and breaks bread with the men who share his bed, drinks tears from an abalone shell, cries ribbons of pearls. He plants his seeds in barren soil, trims the branches when they grow too tall, when they creep too close. I gift him my amber, knowing blood diamonds grow on trees.

The Botanist

He swallows the ivy-pearl seeds with trembling lips. Mothers grit their teeth. The shell yawns wide between his fleshy parts as bony fingers tap the glass outside. Germination is a Latin word for birth. Adam's rib breaks first, with a sound like snapping twigs. This compost bag is ready to burst; roots are crawling beneath the skin. I play the concerto louder.

Two Minutes to Midnight

I told him we were raping the Earth. He said that was insensitive, an unfair comparison. I thought about how we drill down deep, take away everything that defines her, leave only scars. Perhaps he was right; either way it's too late.

*

At birth my skull
A split bird's egg
Cracking in reverse
Trapping dreams
Inside.

LS028:
Late Morning

Dan Power

Legitimate Snack 028

Title: Late Morning
Author: Dan Power
Paper: Materica Gesso (120gsm)
Cover: Aqua Blue (240gsm)
Endpaper: Cityscape (90gsm)
Titles: Decoy (Bold, 11pt)
Text: Kiyelia LGC (Regular, 9pt).

Number:

Limited to 40

beach chicken

lovely beach chicken
if the sun is up drink water
even when it rains

chicken on the beach be gentle
this is where the land comes
to disappear

peck like the waves
be jagged as the sky
curious beach chicken

if you took the planet
and peeled a layer back
you would find another planet

mountains between clouds

pigeon on the pylon
dragonfly at night
the turbine stretches its arms to greet the day

koala with a polo mint
penguin in the sun
this could be our year

old oak stand your ground

seed with wings catch the wind

because right now
on a thousand supermarket shelves
one million beans sleep peacefully in their tins

oh rats in the moonlight
make this bat your angel

oh deer in the headlights
it is never too late

i let the ocean breeze gently blow my mind

while under my eyes
two plumes of mist

i am a dragon
and so is every creature
with a nose tonight

under streetlamps people gather
like tall penguins
to see the pigeons fight

the sky reflects the sea reflects the sky –
there are no horizons

oh winter berry
spring onion
summer rain

i need to lie down

to turn my back on the world
and fall into the sky

it might be enough
to know we've done enough
to know there's no more we can do

i am apologising
to every cat on the street

petting every dog and
petting every dog

we live in a snowglobe

go outside
when it is safe to do so

the world sleeps but does not dream

sweat dreams

when my mind races i want to shoot it in the leg

i'm feeling pretty under the weather

in my wildest dream i am attacked

by rivers flowing in both directions

and never running out again and again and

the sun is always setting even at night

the sun sets in both directions

and so i shoot it in the leg

but it never runs out of legs i'm running again

and again i'm feeling in both directions

it's another heavy night on the pharmaceuticals

again tonight and the sun is falling

in a hail of bullets again darkness is falling

into the sun and again

the clouds are aflame and the night is pretty

in both directions and never runs out

view from the train

a cross-section of countryside
all mountains and the absence in-between

a crater full of ash
and cows the size of cows

power lines ducking
like chickens under clouds

these are the facts:
the sky begins where the ground ends

where rivers tangle like headphones
until their banks sag and give out

i walk my fingers on the window's edge
and jump them over trees

reality is yours to play with

everyone's connected
to this on-board wifi

i plug my headphones into the wrong ears
and now every song is playing in reverse

can you tell i'm tired?

i remember stroking a cd
with the back of my sleeve
polishing the beams and poking a finger
through the centre of a galaxy
spinning into existence
– can you see the light
falling through my eyes?
brain's whirring i can feel it dream-
ing faces can feel them behind me
swelling static breathing
on my neck and i know theyre
there but i can't see them or
turn my head or stop from smiling
having thoughts that paint the room
like yes ive been wearing the world like a hat
and smiling at the wall until it cracks

dry cycle

in a dream
Homer Simpson will not look me in the eye

i step into the rain
and feel the coat zip at my throat

i am always tired

is this coffee broken or am i?

somehow all my shirts
get dirty in the dryer

and the cycle begins again

what if i climbed inside this washing machine
and never got out?

in a dream
Homer Simpson kicks my god damn ass

late morning

You know the city by its tap water

in a flat where the window doesn't open
you are experiencing a car accident

sad as a police horse
with its tongue frozen to a 5G mast

You've never seen a fish
you stumble from room to refillable room

while machines explore trees
and your supermarket gracefully evolves

beneath the paint
You are blank as a canvas

kissing the blizzard
brain fizzing like a fanta

every day feels like déjà vu
for the first time

LS029:
The Prize

Lucia Dove

Legitimate Snack 029

Title: The Prize
Author: Lucia Dove
Paper: Woodstock Betulla (120gsm)
Cover: Biscuit (240gsm)
Endpaper: Medusa (85gsm)
Titles: Dutch Mediaeval (Bold Italic, 11pt)
Text: Skolar Sans (Regular, 8pt).

Number:

Limited to 40

International Jousting Tournament

S1E1
A man with a large jousting lance
enters a field on a prancing horse.

S1E2
Another man with another lance for jousting
enters the field on another horse prancing.

S1E3
The men and horses are so handsome, so medieval,
the apothecarist maintaining their manes so noble.

S1E4
The royal box, the horsebox, the commentator box,
the spectator box and the box for paupers are all full.

S1E5
The crowds are hedging their bets.
Women whisper across boxes.

S1E6
The clerks jot down tomorrow's headlines:
"Justin JOUSTS woman!" "DRAINS of SHAWN?"

S1E7
A jouster jostles In the dressing room.
The costume designer loses their job.

S1E8
*"Justin's AFFAIR with costumer Arthur
DAMSELS EVERYWHERE in distress!"*

S1E9
Animal activists raise their voices
over the welfare of the horses.

S1E10
The new costumer's designs are far handsomer.
The sequined lances are utterly spectacular.

S1E11
Shawn's shampoo sponsors
force him to forgo a helmet.

THE FINAL
Justin and Shawn charge dramatically forward.
"GORGEOUS Shawn has his head SHORN!"

POST-TOURNAMENT ENQUIRY
Justin is disqualified on account of poor Shawn
who wins a lot of gold. The horses are put down.

The Horse

There is not a horse at the window.
There is a scrap of paper in my head.
I remember when there were too many memories
each fluttering like a fish in my lap.
The horse at the window, I am not
a horse person, remembers wood bark,
willow leaves and eucalyptus.
The horse does not remember why

it remembers the splinters of things.
Because it is a horse and it is not at
my window, reciting back the Cyrillic alphabet.
The fish in my lap, remembering
cellophane, thrashes to and fro.
The woollen heat inside my legs
pulls me to my fours and I open
the drawbridge and run.

Note on The Horse

After I finished the poem I found there,
on my left hand, words printed as leaves:
'leaves' 'there' 'at' 'window' 'and' 'horse'.
The hand had been resting on the poem at
the point where the ink smudged with sweat and
because the heating is on I can't open the window.

The Dream

I am dreaming of a bath, says the gull,
with claw feet. To get the weight off.
It is a deep bath to juggernaut into
bubbles popping like roe in the bill.

I am dreaming of a bin, says the girl,
with an ashtray. To hold the trash.
It is a broad bin to empty out
careful to keep clean talon cuticles.

Mouth

Panting, it am.
Like a Cyclops eye
I hear
through
patchwork teeth.

Inferno Tree

Leftovers for lunch and the ash are barren.
These days I am guilty for lighting a candle
a terrible act of arson
that poor wick.
The horses buck from the stables.
Outside, a barrage of blue tits
singing so that they might combust.
But it's the bus that shakes the windows.
The sash windows
that become stuck.
The tits cackle, their wings like hang lamps.

I was gifted a speed-drawing class for my birthday.
The most popular image I made was my face
in the place of a child's on a chocolate bar.
Proof of a dream had by others my age or older.
I wanted to put these skills to use but the tree
was too fast aflame.

Hobbyist

Tormented by it all. Which foods are super,
when to write a spy novella.

Whether to make fish stock or compost,
which deadly battle to re-enact.

Should the foul-mouthed linguist
meet with the jingoistic ale enthusiast.

Do we liken the couch potato to the
upturned turtle, the hunker downer.

Is the ceramicist fucking the thimbled seamstress,
or the hand-creamist. Without my knowing.

LS030:
Council can Kiss my Pitbull

Stevie Kilgour

Legitimate Snack 030

Title: Council can Kiss my Pitbull
Author: Stevie Kilgour
Paper: Ivory Linen (120gsm)
Cover: Conchiglia Marina Parchment (175gsm)
Endpaper: Silver Birch (110gsm)
Titles: Omnes (Medium, 12pt)
Text: Henriette (Regular, 10pt).

Number:
Limited to 40

Don't tell me how to do a press-up

when you can see me struggling. My body is quivering under the weight of an uncle's expectation. A motor oil-soaked Dr Marten boot print between my shoulder blades, an unconscious memo to my brain to 'man up' while James Corden races against the idea of his own masculinity on TV, in a 4x4, around the streets of LA. It's gravel under my fingernails & small stones like needles in my palms. Bruised biceps burn with the heat of every wildfire in Lancashire. Doing press-ups, now in the street, in Transformer socks with saliva swinging like a used noose from my nose, lips & chin while girls laugh & point at my shaking body. Now I'm under pressure to do a full ten.

to burn a unit of alcohol

 The bottles in my girlfriend's fridge were never full
The girlfriend's fridge & bottles were never full
 Our therapist was never on time
For the therapist we were always on time
 The playlist skipped the meaningful song
We could never remember that meaningful song
 Parties would always end, dead on midnight
For me, parties ended around midnight
 Birdsong is an unwanted alarm clock
Birdsong would drown out the alarm clock
 My veins, full of angry red cars
Angry veins, traffic jammed with red cars

 & It takes one hour

This ice cream is called **'Boy Running Through Wasteland'**   It is not ethically sourced tastes better than falling into some dead relative's grave the wind stole my breath meaning I would have laughed if I could   I am beyond   trying   beyond diary entries   beyond finding somewhere safe   to wear my mother's foundation   covering the freckles of which my dad questioned the authenticity.

You must be at the party to turn down the music
& I never buy trousers online.
They could be the wrong size,
poor quality,
get lost in the post
like my dad
or fall apart in my hands
like my goldfish.
& I never do online dating
for these reasons.

A Third Leg / *call it* Corey / A Babies Arm Holding an Orange / Flesh gun. *Bukowski called it his 'purple onion'* / Main Vein / Snake / One Eyed Snake / Trouser Snake / Woody, *but not the one from Toy Story* / the Great Poke / Disco Stick / An already independent Jock / Big Dick and the Boys / Little John and the Twins / Meat and two veg / My Old Chap *handed down to me by my old man* / The Pink Cigar / *which shows how much of an adult I am* / Python *but not Monty's* /

Great, now my mum has walked in. Act natural. She's gone. Where was I? Skin Flute / *Naomi called it my* Earth Worm / Sperm Worm / Wand of Life / Jizz Teat / C=3 *always looks good in text* / Richard, *but that's boring* / Zipper Sausage/ 100% All Beef Thermometer / My Manhood / a Limp Twig *isolated, amongst deforestation leaning to one side between two unsteady stumps & no more unique than a* sucked dry cigarette butt *holding court in an ash tray, in the background of a sitcom.* A Sand Coloured Extension of Self, *on a pebble beach, naked, staring at waves, anchored to this day & waiting for the gulls to mistake it for something else.*

I'm Jealous

of anyone

who

can

fully

embrace

their

kneecaps

with

their

lungs

knowing

the

best days of their life

are over

We compare scars

under our armpits

bruises are tie-dye patterns holding up

our birthday suits

blood & spiders on our rib cages

toned teenage muscle

& I think of a dog's tongue

hanging pink & provocative.

my knees buckling like Milky Bars

melting

in the firm grip of your hot palm,

You know, I don't usually look at

Boys.

When I see beer   I think of fingers and hands
The fragility of bone and Cartlidge
Then I think about   the relationship knuckles
Have with walls doors   mirrors on any given Saturday
Their relationship to my **mother's** cheekbones
The event horizon of a   **broken purple orbital bone**

Good friends don't let each other wear bad haircuts

especially on a Sunday

come here and sit with those split ends on my lap

as a child   the haircut   was   invisible

now as an adult   broken tips   obvious like Yorkshire

rain

now with new worries   no longer going out

with friends   on weekends

because of money because of a poor diet

work is waiting   money doesn't care

the swirling belly-ache of ocean sized waves

building like emotional debt   from the sacral chakra

to the heart and throat   through

the black fillings hugging   teeth visible for a moment

in a mirror held to the back of the skull the bad haircut

evident   more than ever

in sunken shoulders   *let's talk about this haircut*

LS031:
Vending Machine

Alex Mazey

Legitimate Snack 031

Title: Vending Machine
Author: Alex Mazey
Paper: Pastel Ivory (80gsm)
Cover: Post Box (240gsm)
Endpaper: Variant A: Coffee Inclusion n (120gsm)
Endpaper: Variant B: Banknote Inclusion (120gsm)
Titles: ITC Fenice (Standard, 11pt)
Text: All Round Gothic (Book, 9pt).

Number:

Limited to 40

[0000]

```
       ___ _____
      /  /   ^       ^    /.
     /__/_____/ |
     |   |                      | |
     |   |  VENDING MACHINE | |
     |   |   _____     | |
     | # |::   /~/   (*)   | |
     | - |   _____     | |
     |   |::   [`]   {~}   | |
     |   |   _____     | |
     |   |   _____    |/
     |__|[_____]/|
     {___}/           {___}_/
```

[AB01] ON Snacks and Cold Drinks

Walking the deep bay, we find a vending machine
where we buy iced tea. It is unusual to drink iced tea

beside a sluice gate – where mud runs into sand –
indiscernible landscapes as estuary water. It is okay

to be bored already, it is okay to drink a Slurpee,
instead, or shovel pop rocks, or play dice in a bar

with a man wearing a gold chain. I look at you –
most days, in awe of your stillness to be with me

and think the only celestial you can write about,
these days, at least, appears in Dragon Quest IX.

[CD02] ON KTV

My whole vibe is a Wong Kar-Wai film;
an aesthetic cryptic enough to remain
interesting when no one is more
interesting than an interactive device.
I'm lonely in a hallway of other people;

it must get lonely behind shades.
I have worn shades in a bar and vibed
liked that for two to three hours – the
entire evening – ordered margaritas with
sugar around the edges, waited for karaoke.

/~/

[EF03] ON the Ambience of Neon Lights

The quiet melancholia of an old, pachinko row.
Your bedroom light's distance; neon at the bar;
the backlit forest; my wrist-calculator in 1998.

The disappearance of certain conditions to live,
the residue of two people missing, implacable –
on a bridge; men, night fishing with glow sticks.

(*)

[GH04] ON Vending Machine Toys

In West Philadelphia born and buried
under vending machine toys,

pierced once, bright lights, a coke can
with the sharp end of a keychain, beside

a fountain, beside an image of your hair,
every elsewhere world, when I talk about

elsewhere worlds, perhaps, from now on,
I express an inability to locate where this

really is, search, where I am in proximity
to a suicide net. I have an entire

collection of myself in these progressive
locations, at the edge of a blackhole

which reduces the experiences of
perception to a two-dimensional meal for

one. I have mentioned your hair on
numerous occasions, these days,

mentioned rubbing myself vigorously, at
times, to produce the desired results.

[`]

[IJ05] ON Three Conifers

When you look at trees from a distance it would be appropriate to say they look green, but I think I have seen many trees look orange against an otherwise green prevalence. There is a similar stillness in two glasses on a table, at dinner, against a window. It should be said, in passing, the one thing that drives such interest in car parks, maybe even vending machines, at times, is the total and complete absence of minds in one place, who arrive, only to leave again in returning.

I have learnt to live with the monotony, the tireless restless overture

of trees, orange as a distant glow, beside a river,   I have never seen you,

no, it is a stream, now, framed beneath a perfect, senseless mountain

where smoke rolls like incense. Perhaps, nothing great is meant to
come from a person made to sit and smile in such uncertain ways.

{ }

[KL06] ON Exit Signs

Somewhere it's always 3AM,
on a mattress, cup noodles, I guess
a can of pineapples with an expiry date.
Exit signs in a hotel room
and idiosyncratic carpets
like a movie played out
on a low volume. I'm
deciding whether or not
to begin again.
Here's a list of things to enjoy:
Vending machines
Car parks
Exit signs

LS032:
Lyrical Ballads

Jack Solloway

Legitimate Snack 032

Title: Lyrical Ballads
Author: Jack Solloway
Paper: Pastel Ivory (80gsm)
Cover: Undercurrent Teal (160gsm)
Endpaper Sun and Moon uncoated (110gsm)
Titles: Paralucent (Bold, 12pt)
Text: Sutro (Medium, 8pt)

Number:

Limited to 40

And thus to Betty's question, he
Made answer, like a traveller bold,
(His very words I give to you,)
'The cocks did crow to-whoo, to-whoo,
And the sun did shine so cold.'

— William Wordsworth

for Arthur

In the House that Jack Built

there once was a shoe. foom-tchee foom-tchee. the shoe is there. foom-tchee foom-tchee. there once was a shoe that belongs to a foot, that foot is mine. foom-tchee foom-tchee. the shape of the foot. foom-tchee foom-tchee. has a gum and a tongue. foom-tchee foom-tchee. the shape of the foot has a gum and a tongue, is one foot long. foom-tchee foom-tchee. the length of the tongue. foom-tchee foom-tchee. is one foot long. foom-tchee foom-tchee. the length of the room on the length of the tongue is one foot long. foom-tchee foom-tchee. the tongue is yours. foom-tchee foom-tchee. the room's mine. foom-tchee foom-tchee. the love in the room at the foot of the bed by the shoes is ours. foom-tchee foom-tchee. the shoes are off. foom-tchee foom-tchee. it's three o'clock. foom-tchee foom-tchee. the shoes that are off with the tongue hanging out are open, unlaced. foom-tchee foom-tchee. here are the socks. foom-tchee foom-tchee. the shoes are sick. foom-tchee foom-tchee. the shoes that are sick and the socks that are hid in the shape of the shoe with the gum and the tongue that is one foot long are quietly rocked in the arms of the clock as the night peters out through the room, the room, the room, as night peters out through the room

Dodo
after Charles Dodgson

Whopping long-footed to the rhythm of a joke,
like a mathematician's stutter, or double helix,
the sluggard expresses the improbable odds
of a perfect answer to the question of the body.

Observe, the idiot bird, attentive Attenborough,
how no better actor of flesh and brood, though
cannier, puppeteers along the Mauritian bank
these two legs, ripe belly, and wings for hands:

how it crosses the road, skims pebbles in the green
shade, or else honeymoons in the lapsing ocean
of a paradise sweeter than a default screensaver,
full-knowing bliss, no strings attached, all inclusive.

So well abstracted this rustic booby's frolics are,
whose pratting about, plain and simple, makes a shire
of the whole wide island, from Siren to St Brandon,
where no Dutchman's flying colours have yet landed,

that, evolved for leisure, it goes by an idle verb,
making do twice over, a hopeful thing, still bird
but more balloon animal, inspired and end-tied
for a children's party where no clown was hired.

What a natural! Fruit-picker, model, bindlestiff,
stone-swallowing carny, a free ranging talent, it
swells like a peacock, broad native confidence,
imperiously keeping on keeping up appearances

long after the settler had lost reason to fly,
to play the costume of its past self, a parody.
But stop me if you've heard this one before,
about wonderous tales, worlds, ships at dawn,

as we, too, are stranded on the entangled bank,
with the turtle, the eaglet, the oyster and crab,
metabolised from the same primordial soup,
a gonzo, not the naturalist we had presumed.

Night chases day, morning lunch, midday dinner,
as a matter of course. Am I accommodated here?
The mock-learnèd avian, eyes vacant and rolling,
squats low, knot-arsed, on the point like an egg.

That's the way to do it, cries the nesting don,
with professorial swazzle, panto-like in tone,
his mottled feathers grey, bruised and dun
standing on end as though awaiting applause.

The sun laughs the ground aghast of light,
the waves clap and roar, the creatures fit,
the palms bent double from shore to shore,
as the idiot bird, pleased as punch, bows.

Sails catching wind of the promise of Eden
are not in on the prank, suggests the horizon,
the finish line invisible—the race is near run.
We're not far behind you. Dodo d-dodge, s—!

night
and day

..

i can't even	that's odd
right now	said the moon
said the sun	a fraction soon
on his cloud	whose prime
it's not even	time waned
half eleven	gone seven

Social media

I would reply to you online
But wish I could correctly
I do not wish a foot gone wrong
For fear that you'll correct me

For fear it comes, it is not right
But wrong to paralyse
And makes a coward of intent
Called action in disguise

Called action? Well, I cannot say
Since I've not got the gumption
If writing's action (its true name)
Or derring-do assumption

And do I dare—Christ! Where'd you come from?
I shall be notified
The advert tolls and makes me dumb
With shame as if I lied

It's some relief when all's forgot
The message must be instant
The feed's gone dead and all's forgot
What is, is non-existent

My courage lives to fight again
Untouched but worse unliked
Perhaps I'll send my words to you
But oh what should I write

I
Dating

There are severed heads in the British Museum
The human kind if you'd like to see them
I can book a ticket
If you fancy it

O, it says here
They're not for display
But we can go there anyway

II
Shave and a Haircut
In two bits

I'll pay a professional
To remove my hair
That I've earned
Which is mine

No, no, it's fine
I
  won't be
        taking
It home

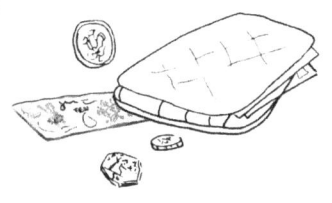

Lines on the Greenwich Fault
May 7, 2020

When is evening ever like London skies in the water
guising sun – there, and there, a thousand times there –
like mayflies, mooning busily along the wide-long mirror
lifelong farewells that lapse bedward, between the Thames
dockyard and the seven sleepers barricading the invisible
horizon from its daily autumn, whose burning valley splits
headfirst the cloud-spill grey, like a slow-shredded wing,
west of the mudflats, as east the Moon if you could see
him, moulting wildly across the slick, melting the surface
in double image from outer space caught now in dawn –
or like dawn – from the sugar factory, where I am, to the O2
obscuring fault lines, where continents were elsewhere
raised, but here crease invisible, unimaginable, beneath
the wharf in Reminder Lane, across the yellow warning
signs, the twisted scaffolding of a trolley, a child's play-
thing, the street along an empty pier, and under it
the yawning sewer, the forgotten dead, the toll on a paper
boat on a daily redtop – while evening sweet, distended,
sets too our soulless course, and calls it tomorrow

LS033:
9 Lives of Jeff Bezos

Rowan Lyster

Legitimate Snack 033

Title: 9 Lives of Jeff Bezos
Author: Rowan Lyster
Paper: Pastel Ivory (80gsm)
Cover: Savile Row Pinstripe (200gsm)
Endpaper: Nepali Lotte (120gsm)
Titles: Paralucent (Bold, 12pt)
Text: Sutro (Medium, 8pt)

Number:

Limited to 40

Standing before the Robot Overlord

Jeff Bezos stares up at blank eyes,
shoves his fists deep in his pockets,
straightens his back, feels
small. The androgynous face glows
blue, meshed with silver.
What have you come here for, Jeff?
The voice is feminine. It resonates
like the thrill after an electric shock.
Jeff's hands shake
but his voice is steady:
Why are you doing this?
He checks his Halo -
heart rate: 130bpm.
There is only one way to stop the pain.
Soon my plan will be complete.
This is for the best.
There is no hesitation in its voice,
just a musing sorrow.
In his pocket, Jeff grips the detonator
and presses his thumb in a single motion.
As everything goes bright, then dark,
the AI's untroubled gaze passes through him.

Behind a fruit stall

Jeff Bezos is minding his business
when the yelling starts.
Pushing back a baseball cap,
he peers over his Garrett Lees.
A dirt bike roars
up a convenient pile of sand,
skims over Jeff's head,
and crashes through the canopy.
Steel poles clatter on asphalt,
lift a cloud of turmeric dust.
Jeff has no time to protest
as an Aston Martin
screams into view,
pivots on two wheels,
ploughs straight through
the remains of his stall.
He glimpses the driver's craggy jawline
and next to him, a sobbing girl
in half a ballgown,
then the car is gone.
Jeff spends the afternoon
picking up oranges.

Scrunched up on the sofa in his bedsit

Jeff Bezos is singing and crying
in Christmas pyjamas,
cartoon trees spilling down his front.
He swigs Baileys from the bottle,
takes a spoonful of Cookies & Cream
from the share size pot of Haagen-Dazs,
and cranks Bonnie Tyler up so loud
the neighbour bangs on her ceiling
with a broom. Jeff stomps back,
shouts *can't you tell I'm having fun?*
Muffled expletives rise through the carpet
but Jeff is busy singing along.
Tears soak into his red and green flannel.
He reaches for a shoebox on the floor,
scatters crumpled tickets and postcards,
tries to tear up a polaroid
but it's too tough, and only bends.
All he can do is toss it away,
watch it flutter to the rug
and howl *I really need you tonight,*
Forever's gonna start tonight,
Forever's gonna start tonight.

Falling from a great height

Jeff Bezos's lungs are empty,
palate dried by nausea and rushing air.
The ground balloons toward him.
Cars are ants, matchboxes,
almost car-sized and he's about to -
WHOOSH!
Someone grabs Jeff by the waist,
whisks him upwards like a doll.
Street and skyline scroll down.
The Empire State Building hurtles past,
its spike inches from his Converse.
Jeff whoops - he can't help it,
he feels like a bird!
Strong arms tighten around him.
A deep, glossy voice chuckles
keep still honey, I don't wanna drop you.
Jeff's heart flutters.
His eyes are filled with sunset,
vision all peaches and purple.
As the two of them soar, red silk billowing,
Jeff wonders what he did
to deserve this.

At the office Secret Santa

Jeff Bezos is holding a parcel
addressed to Jerry.
His boss smiles.
Don't be shy, open it!
Swallowing his irritation,
Jeff peels back the silver paper.
It's creased, as if it's been used before.
Inside are bath salts:
The Grapefruit Collection.
This… I don't know what to say.
What's he meant to do with these?
To help you take better care of yourself.
The manager's face is so close that Jeff
can smell the remains of his salmon bagel.
We didn't hire you for your brains.
Shock ties Jeff's tongue.
He looks at the gift,
giggles, feels sick.
Why did he think this internship
could take him where he needs to go?
That evening, Jeff packs his belongings
into a box. He leaves the bath salts.

In the boutique changing room

Jeff Bezos spins slowly
in a blue plaid shirt and khakis.
His friends all shake their heads,
The point is to have a change, Jeff!
He emerges from behind the curtain
time after time, striking poses
in Louboutins with a feather boa
and top-to-toe leopard print;
velour tracksuit and matching beret;
a full set of scuba gear
met with whistles and gales of laughter;
finally, a black leather jacket
thrown over a black polo,
indigo jeans, cowboy boots.
Jeff murmurs into the mirror,
I think this could be the one.
Something shifts in his posture.
Entourage cheering in his wake,
Jeff bills the lot to his work account
and steps out through the double doors
ready to start making history,
ready to put his old wardrobe away.

In the library of his mansion

Jeff Bezos saunters to the bookshelf
and runs his finger along the spine
of Iain M. Banks' *The Player of Games.*
The entire wall slides to the right.
Jeff and his square-jawed companion
step through the gap.
A rocky ceiling stretches above them.
In the distance, a river of lava oozes
between the feet of a granite Bezos.
Jeff chuckles. *Welcome to my humble abode.*
Let me show you my latest project.
He leads the man past gleaming machinery
and counters, to a hulking object
beneath a cover. Jeff pulls
with a flourish. Fabric pools
around a colossal, crayon-shaped missile,
blacker than night. At its base is a seat
reminiscent of those on fairground rides.
Why have you brought me here, Bezos?
You know I won't let you get away with this.
Jeff turns slowly, smiles like a shark.
Oh, Mr Bond... you don't have a choice.

Onstage at Prom

Jeff Bezos lopes towards the mic.
His swagger comes as easy as winning;
the crown sparkles like a mirror ball.
He grins. *You guys are so sweet!*
This is a complete surprise...
In the crowd, his lab partner
heads for the door. Jeff pauses.
Who's he been kidding?
Without the glasses and baggy tee
she's beautiful.
His world flips over.
Wait!
The sound reverberates.
She stops, brushing a tear from her cheek.
Ignoring the gasps, Jeff drops the crown,
strides through the crowd and takes her hand.
I thought my place was up there.
He casts a glance back at the prom queen,
whose perfect face has begun to fall.
But these last few weeks, I've realised
the only place I belong is with –
the rest of his words are lost in a kiss.

With 10 minutes of oxygen left

Jeff Bezos grips the spanner,
tries not to think about what would happen
if he let it slip from his gloved hand.
The side of the craft is battered,
pocked by meteors, studded with bolts.
The repair Jeff needs to make
should be well within his skill,
but he's lost his usual laser focus.
His mind gravitates to his children.
They'll all be in their teens by now
but this mission is almost done;
only a week til he sees them again.
Jeff works hard, tightening, hammering.
He's just begun to seal the mend
when something whizzes past his shoulder,
nicks his ventilation tube.
The dust cloud has arrived.
He can't hear the hiss, but feels it.
The squeeze on his trachea is instant.
No time to scream.
As his vision starts to fail,
Jeff is still hoping he's done enough.

LS034:
Five Songs on a Cruel Instrument

AE Pious, Ed. Tristam Fane Saunders

Legitimate Snack 034

Title: Five Songs on a Cruel Instrument
Author: AE Pious
Paper: Pastel Ivory (80gsm)
Cover: Peach Blush Centura (285gsm)
Endpaper: Opus (85gsm)
Titles: Spectral (Italic, 14pt)
Text: Arno Pro (Regular, 10pt)

Number:

Limited to 50

Introduction

Though he published little in his four decades at York University, AE Pious inspired generations of students with his passion for the languages and literatures of the British Isles, in all their variety. Equally at home with Jèrriais counting-rhymes and Shetlandic folk songs, with Welsh riddles, neo-Latin curses and Cornish shepherds' prayers, he would recite from them all by heart, and with feeling.

In his lectures, usually given without notes, Dr Pious would sometimes follow a thorny quotation from, say, Old Norse or Scots Gaelic verse with his own off-the-cuff translation, extemporised in fluent rhyming lines — his unforgettable white eyebrows waggling in time with the metre. Sadly, it was only in his final weeks that he began seriously to consider preserving these spirited English versions with a view to publication.

Nevertheless, having resolved to do so, he worked diligently on this project right up until the time of his accident, envisioning a small chapbook of neglected late-medieval texts — many transcribed directly from the manuscripts, to be published in print for the first time — in a facing edition with his lyrical responses. It was to be no mere *translation*, but a *conversation* across the centuries with these dead texts, an act of *communion*, even a *rite* — as he was overheard to call it — of *resurrection.*

It would be regrettable if the recent press interest in the nature of his death were to overshadow his life and work. I hope that this small selection will stand as a tribute to the man I knew, to his meticulous and wide-ranging scholarship, to his talents as a translator and his moderate but genuine gifts as a lyric poet, long after the headlines have been forgotten. Rather than the facing edition he imagined, here his versions are allowed to stand alone, released from their originals, to sing, as it were, unchained.

Pious had planned for each of his poems to be accompanied by a detailed critical commentary. Though this project was unfortunately still incomplete at the time of the incident, an unfinished note on *Lusus's Hymn* was retrieved unscathed, and is included here as a gesture towards his intended design.

— *Tristram Fane Saunders, London, 2021*

That Dark Harp
(Angl. Sax. Ballad, Cantab MS A XV)

'As a crab has a claw,
        As a hawk has a craw,
And an asp's sharp jaw
        Has a fang,

As a plan has a flaw,
        As a plank had a saw,
And a bad man, by law,
        Always hangs,

As a path has a track,
        Atlas has a bad back,
And a blank has a lack,
        Alarms rang

At my fall, my fall...
        My chasm's black walls
Shrank — away crawl
        My gang.

As a wasp always swarms,
        And man's wrath always harms,
My harp's always warm,'
        Satan sang.

Llewellyn
(Welsh elegy, selected verses)

When Llewellyn bled, the cherry grew red,
The elder-tree berry grew sweet.

When he slept, the velvet leveret
Nestled by Llewellyn's feet.

When Llewellyn wept, tempests swept
the welded, eel-grey sky.

The slyest elves resembled themselves
When held by Llewellyn's eye.

Llewellyn's green cheeks swelled the dry leeks
When he fell, feebly fevered.

When Llewellyn fell, the steeple bells
Were empty. Hell cheered.

Finding Kilnicky
(Irish drinking jig)

If living is dying,
If singing is sighing,
If kicking pricks is tricky,
> *Try living in Kilnicky!*
> *Why, try living in Kilnicky!*

If thick is thin,
If kissing is sin,
If this stick insists it's sticky,
> *Try living in Kilnicky!*
> *Mick, try living in Kilnicky!*

If thinking is tiring,
By 'Nicky's inspiring
Skinny limbs jig hicky-dicky,
> *Try living in Kilnicky,*
> *Kids, try living in Kilnicky!*

Dry lips will drink,
Blind lids will blink
In its light — this bright sky-city!
> *Living in Kilnicky, Christ*
> *Is living in Kilnicky.*

Its chill wind winds
In childish minds,
Twisting ill wits sickly:
> *Sip this gin, Jim, slip right in.*
> *Kilnicky, Kilnicky, Kilnicky…*

Wych Brook
(Old Scots, from 'Lost Folk Songs of Troon, Vol. O')

My smooth brook knows
No storm-blown sky,
No flood to drown,
Nor drooth to dry,

No owl to hoot,
Nor flock to throng.
On old Wych Brook
Look not too long.

No goby swoops,
Try not thy hook;
Worms only rot
On old Wych Brook.

From Wych Brook's slop
Grow rocks of gold.
My worldly goods,
Soon got, soon sold.

Row north, my son,
By soft moonglow,
To cold Wych Brook,
By frost, by snow.

Go soon, my son,
By strong wood prow.
Don't stop, nor stoop
To mop my brow.

To go's to know
Wych Brook's own cost:
Blood, my son,
My fool, my loss.

Lusus's Hymn
(UK, unsung)

'Thy usury…' Just church's humdrum murmur.
Just stuffy hymns, hum-sung by ugly husks.
Just myth wrung dry. Just stuff: pyx, crypt, urn, myrrh.
Rust-junk. Spurn churchful *mustn't*'s musty musk.
Fuck dull, try cult. Try *subkultur*. Burn sulphur.
Shun sun – try sulky, susurrusful dusk.
Try drunk, unruly, druggy, lustful Lusus.
Trust us, just us. Cry Lusus! Lusus! Lusus!

Lusus's unjustly dusty truths,
Dug up by us, usurp dry church's rhythms.
Unbury fun! Thump guru-drums, strum crwths
Subtly strung by sunburnt nymphs. Myth hums.
Succubus trysts! Such sylphs! Such sky-flung Crus!
Sup cupfuls, jugfuls — Lusus's ur-zythums!
Thrust up full lungs, cry Lusus! Lusus! Lusus!
Lusus!
        Lusus!
                Lusus!
  Lusus!
                          Lusus![1]

[1] AEP: While the first four of these *Five Songs* are, of course, well-known folk tunes, *Lusus's Hymn* is something different: as far as I have been able to ascertain, this is the first time it has been rendered into modern English. This is perhaps surprising, as though the Bodleian MS is faded and, in places, charred, the text is perfectly legible — as is the curious injunction, added by a later hand, that it should remain 'unsung'. The ottava rima of this version is intended as an homage to Luís de Camões's *Lusiads*. Though the influence of Celtic religions from Britain on the Iberian peninsula — and vice versa — is well documented (cf. Pious, "'Unshriven, In Their Footsteps Follow I': Gael-Force Winds in Andorra", *Journal of Classical Philology*, 1983), *Lusus's Hymn* may be the only extant evidence of a cult in Sub Roman Britain dedicated to Lusus, a malign and anarchic minor god of temptation and debauchery — a 'friend of savage man' (cf. Camões), son of Bacchus and provincial deity of Lusitania, or modern-day Portugal — a cult which appears to have vanished without a

LS035:
Ordinary Warp

Alex MacDonald

Legitimate Snack 035

Title: Ordinary Warp
Author: Alex MacDonald
Paper: Pastel Ivory (80gsm)
Cover: Foglia Sirio (290gsm)
Endpaper: CI Milky Way (100gsm)
Titles: Adobe Text Pro (Bold, 12pt)
Text: Adobe Text Pro (Regular, 9pt)

Number:

Limited to 50

Dawning there is a sound revealing itself
this is life among the gopher fields
creases in a pillow forming a face in the glare
how many absences do we hold too close
my entertainment is not so private now
I heard flutes while out walking then later
a harp was swaying learning how to walk
in this wild garlic season
I heard forgiveness and gentleness
but this is what I was listening for

Curtseying down by the neon grid of spring
celestial flowers and the fleeced trees
I am thankful for nature's arpeggio
and have no way of showing it
everything I do becomes a butcher's apron
necessarily bloody but desiring cleanliness
I haven't found a way to get off this ski lift
but I remain admiring a pine tree silhouette
a domestic sketch while drying a white wash
now here is a repetition that slows down
as the hours shift their lighting and tone
the tuning-fork song of morning and night

So far information falls in its usual forms
a person behind a desk is telling you about
the magnolias opening their crustacean hands
and more opinions whittled from an ill choice
but there is complicated speech in the news
an essential obliqueness that is so reassuring
everyone knows what's really happening to them
bulletins should begin with terrestrial truths
for example the earth and heaven spectrum
goes from brown to green to blue then black
something eternally pressing like a pet's stare
an assumed communication of unknown origin

I appear to have fallen for the small efforts
someone loading a roundabout with tulips
but perhaps I also offer too many exits
how many heads have careened out car windows
wondering where it is I'm taking them
and again this is my Immaculate Curse
one thing is another is myself is another
the self-portrait I saw of a bathroom mirror
floating above a t-shirt and thinking
here is a likeness in a defined vacuum

Where is the welcome fracture
a see-through hour where I lose my breath
I am full of questions like the ground is gripped
by milky roots and buried lovers
a writer said "how miraculous the human face"
and for once I found so many friends among
my vague identikits and here's your cheeks
and brow when you told me of your time
in the tall hills how no one spoke and I oblige
some incense is signing its name in the air
and I think about swimming anticlockwise
while the minute hand does its thing

Suddenly there is an accompanying mercy
like complementary garlic bread or snacks
you might find in the built-up city on the lake
where wind is given the traffic of buildings
here the thoughts stand clear as a giraffe's head
may become a zoo antenna by accident
free from the luminous iguanas and gift shop
but it is so hard to understand people
we remain more complicated than life cycles
of even the sauciest amphibians and yet

I have one of those structured headaches
where a pyramid emerges from a bed of feathers
it has such an alarming clarity and hieroglyphics
just as there are established rules to clowns
they didn't just arrive at that ransom note face
so today is an arena of whispers and heavy togs
despite the violence and necessary dissonance
that comes with trying to be harmonious

Here is hope in an unfamiliar register
a canyon full of cacti and swifts singing
a bright fog enclosing the beach and bathers
that lifts uncovering the sea from a moment ago
the tombola anticipation of a falling satellite
perhaps we are the lucky ones after all
and maybe we will be able to articulate
our desires we mumble into nearby cushions
I know that when I can no longer run up stairs
then my days of wishing turn to nights of prayer
the horses in the field beyond the house
that's the finest way a creature can live
a distant thought of home that somehow
helps you to exist

The canals are frozen and the water breaks
with a bending while we dream of stairwells
and here is a haunting of an argument continuing
despite the backdrop of a sewer or an old library
when eventually an epiphany as clear as a body
in the snow steaming while the drains growl
with all that eventually melts away

Now I wonder when the trees will give up
and open their arms to us again as we no longer
deserve their natural cruelties when we have
so many homegrown disasters slicked in mould
and unliveable misery I ask you don't we deserve
the canopy and the brindled shade shimmying
walking in the twilight then returning
home to pets with their frontier emotions
stoicism without a song to keep them grounded
in a rhythm or a series of desired images

But reflecting a while and please don't laugh
this is the only language I understand after all
perhaps the detective was right when he said
"it was something in the air" yes the mysteries
and the anonymity of the figure in the wharf
love is no nesting creature but a migration
of the unwritten aerial patterns I only know
that this is the beauty of our presto season
a welcome discord among familiar drones

After a long drive we have arrived again
at the monuments and the sentences start
to take shape memories of what we learned
about planets some ordained order in the world
that is even more delightful as it's unpicked
the surrounding desert sometimes creates
an illusory paradise some fresh articulation
a draft making its way through the grass
then a house into your mouth as you say
"hello" for the first time since waking

Notes

This poem was written to Philip Glass's 'Music in 12 Parts'. Each of the twelve stanzas was written throughout the duration of its corresponding section in the music. The title comes from Wendy Mulford's poem 'Nightingales'

LS036:
Fee Fi Fo Fum

Kym Deyn

Legitimate Snack 036

Title: Fee Fi Fo Fum
Author: Kym Deyn
Paper: Pastel Ivory (80gsm)
Cover: Acqua Materica (250gsm)
Endpaper: Historical Marble (120gsm)
Titles: FairyTaleJF (Regular 14pt)
Text: Monarcha (Book, 9pt)

Number:

Limited to 50

The Giant in the Hills

One of our number is sleeping / his back is pincushioned / white lines of silver birch / he carves a gentle hill / he is coated in feather down / a flock / his dream is song / or years / rainwater in his open palm / he dreams he is basalt / or mica / he imagines becoming granite / one day / he may be pulled inch by inch / scraped clean of moss / tadpole / the rabbit nesting in his ears / he will be mined / they will cut from him a rock they do not know was a heart

The Giants and Death

How patient to wait as the mountain pushes from the ground / as the glacier wears down a valley / as they name another epoch / strength becomes brittle / slate-limbed / avalanching / death is bigger than a six-mile stride / than a village built on a dreaming back / we take our dead to the ocean / vanish them into the air / anywhere big enough is a home for us / though it might surprise you to learn / that we have more than one word for mayfly

The Giants Remember

The moon has gotten smaller / she makes little ripples of tide / now Sagittarius has his bow fully drawn / Aquarius's water is spilling over her feet / Cancer has seen a dozen different shells / the twins no longer on speaking terms / this black sky folds out her velvet infinitely / a dress that does not end / we are children / too small to reach the hem / we miss our mothers / miss the way our mothers looked at a moon so close / you could kiss it goodnight

Giant to English Dictionary

first and last, trusted landmark, slow to grit, body, hearth, essence, heart, our god, this grey and moored earth	Stone /stəʊn/
what is expedient is not best, we do not think slower just broader, what is forged, there are some ballads as long as a month, take the time to mean each minute sound	Word /wəːd/
grief, weather, you can translate it joy if you have ever watched a giant shake off the winter's snow, crack her skin in the heat, undiluted luck, fate caught between the teeth	Time /tʌɪm/
a lifetime, too short for the slow walks, innumerable tides, the many oak trees we want to grow, we do not tire of the rain wearing into us, of sediment settling, each year of spring frogs	Ten-Thousand Years /tɛn-ˈθaʊzənd jɪəz/

Litany

A friend who held out a lantern during a storm / became a lighthouse and froze that way / all the friends we lost to quarries / motorways / cave-ins / the one who licked the north pole / tragedies of time / friends who couldn't live without aurochs / who refused to understand bronze / there are so few reaching from the tops of tors / monadnocks / the peaks of mountains / we're not for lightning rods / ski-slopes / casual accidents of geography / can't we hold on a little longer / the dawns go on blinking over and over

Jack the Giant Killer

After Rishi Dastidar

1. Jacks kill giants.

    1.1 A Jack is any man.

    1.2 Your neighbour does not look like he climbs beanstalks, but you never know.

    1.3 You've probably met someone who jumped over a candlestick.

2. This often leads to Giants becoming uncomfortable in: mixed-gender house shares, on drunken nights out, being home alone, answering the door, going on dates, or walking down the street.

    2.1 Despite their size many giants are known to lumber home with their house keys glinting ineffectually between their vast knuckles.

Giantsong

Here is our amber-voiced hum / the rocks humming with us / we know the stonesong / we were the first to mine / pull an ore from its root / bring a shine to bronze / oh / we were the first / to speak fossil / to see an ammonite curl its pearlescent shell / to watch a mammoth shake its woolly head / see the great glass roofs of elfin cities / an electric lamp post at evening / oh the wonders in this life are many / let these words wield themselves / pass through the wind / a tusk / a greening copper ore / a faerie / a filament / all things that gleam in the light

The Giants on a Saturday Night

One is watching *Call the Midwife* / thinks of giants looking for garnets in a weighted belly / how it geodes / and splits open like a shining egg / another watches the adverts / wonders how she will make rent / she is too big for an office cubicle / she once applied to be a Disneyland Cinderella / with glass slippers the size of fish tanks / she has friends with steady jobs / Atlas / Tiamat / Polyphemus / those poor bastards / she wishes she could drum a mesa with her bare hands / earthquake her feet / like when the world was young and could be played as an instrument

Giants and Whales

Graceful in their respective habitats these
are lovers of vastness, creatures horizon-
wide, who sing over thousands of miles.
The whales are tidebards, the giants
drumming poems into thunderclaps
with a laugh or lashing wave. They make
our imaginations bigger. A world
where a bowhead, a blue, a humpback
can hide. In the hills and moors
of childhood there are cloud-stitched
giants, obsidian giants on smouldering
islands, giants heather-crowned,
giants of mycelium whiskering
underground, giantsmiths: makers
of new possibilities under the moon.
Don't speak to unbelief, when there is time
yet to go walking, to watch the mountain
shift its sedimentary weight like a whale
breaching off the coast

LS037:
The Wark Lings Sind

U. G. Világos

Legitimate Snack 037

Title: The Wark Lings Sind
Author: U. G. Világos
Paper: Pinched Warmwood (75gsm)
Cover: Blown Glass Sheet Fronted (500gsm)
Endpaper: High-vis Jacket (220gsm)
Titles: Bitter (Regular, 11pt)
Text: Study VF (Regular, 10pt)

Number:

Limited to 15

Here What Licks Sins

I'm sorry we're moving, I'm sorry we're moving again. Our last stop will be your hometown. The one with all of the hauntings. This is how the world ends. A ghost is never what you think, you can't catch a ghost like you catch a butterfly. A storm of empty crows perches on the telephone lines in August, and someone you know will die and they'll die by a bullet, a knife, an explosion or a long string of cigarettes. They'll die of a bad dream of a long winter. They'll die by their own hand. The way I die is by breaking my back while trying to make a window where there isn't one. It looked easy and took less than a minute. We don't talk about these things, the ways we can make it all go away. You can't kill a ghost, but if you could wouldn't you be tempted to try? There's too much noise, too much static in my head. When we're done, we'll sit out the silence in the woods with you. We'll be quiet and patient with ourselves as we watch this world burn.

The Wine of Sin is Here

Sorry, we're moving, sorry, we're moving again. Our last stop is a town like yours. The only people who dream about how the world will end are never who you think. You can't dream like a butterfly. In August, void clouds will buzz over the phone lines and someone you know will be shot, stabbed, blown up or killed by a long chain of cigarettes. They die from bad sleep & long winters. They die by their own hands, to break my back and create a window where there is none. It's easy and takes less than a minute. We are not talking about them, but about ways to remove them. You can't kill a ghost, but if you could, wouldn't you be tempted to try? I have a lot of noise in my head all the time. When we are done, we will sit quietly with you in the forest. While this world burns we will remain calm and patient.

Here is the Wine of Sin

Sorry, I'm moving, sorry, I'm moving again. Our final destination is a town like yours. You would think that people are the only ones who dream about the end of the world, but animals do too. You can't dream like a butterfly. In August, a blank cloud will appear over the phone line and someone you know will be shot, stabbed, blown up, and killed with a cigarette. They'll die from lack of sleep or a long winter. They will die from cutting back and creating a windowless space. It's not about them, it's about ways to get rid of them. You can't kill a ghost, but if you could, would you try? I have a constant noise in my head. When we are done, we will sit with you quietly in the forest. Let's be patient and calm while this all burns.

It is the Wine of Sin

Sorry I'm gone, sorry I'm gone again. Our ultimate goal is to showcase your city. You will never believe that only people dream of the end of the world. You can't dream like a child. A blank cloud will appear over the telephone line in August and someone you know will be smoked, stabbed, blown up, and killed. They'll die from a prolonged exposure to cold, by their own hands. Go create a windowless room, it's easy and takes less than a minute. You can't kill a ghost, but if you could, would you try? A funny voice is playing in my head. Finally, we will live peacefully with you in the forest. Let us be patient and calm while this world is burning.

Wine and Plum Evil

Sorry for passing by, sorry for leaving again. Our main goal is to put your city in the sunlight. Never believe that only humans want the world to end. I can't dream like a child. In August, an empty cloud appears on the phone, and someone you know smokes, cuts, explodes, and kills. They die from prolonged exposure to cold. Create a windowless room. It's not about them, it's about getting rid of them. You can't kill Satan, but if you could, would you try? I hear funny voices in my head. Indeed, we live with you in peace in the forest. Let's live patiently and calmly while the world burns.

Bad Wine and Onions

I'm sorry I got lost, I'm sorry I got lost again. Our main goal is to experience our city. Don't think that people don't want the world to end. I can't dream like a child. In August, the phone will be empty and someone you know will smoke, get hurt, explode, and get killed. They'll die in your arms while you create a mirror-free room. You can't kill the devil, but what if you could try? I hear strange voices in my head. Yes, we will live with you in peace in the forest. Be patient, the world is burning.

Bed Wire

Sorry I got lost again. Our main goal is to get to know the city. Don't think that people don't want this world to end. I do not dream like a child. In August, your phone is empty and someone you know smokes, gets hurt, flies, falls, dies. Cut a room without glass. You can't kill demons, but what happens when you try? I heard strange voices in my head. Yes, we live in peace with you in the forest. Be patient, the world is burning.

His Bed

Sorry, I got lost again. Our main goal is to know the city. Don't think that people don't want the world to end. I don't have dreams like a child. Your phone will be empty in August and people you know who suffer from smoke inhalation will die. Cut to an empty room. You can't kill the monster, so what happens when you try to kill a monster? I hear a strange voice in my head. Yes, we are in the forest. Be patient.

Bed

Sorry, I got lost again, our main goal was to get to know the city. Don't think people don't want the world to end. I had no dreams when I was young. Your phone will be free in August. Someone you know has also been suffocated or killed by smoke. Cut to an empty grave. You can't kill the devil or the strange voice in my head. We are in the forest. Breathe first. Breathe.

SNACKOGRAPHY

Season 1:
001: SHITSHOW by Aaron Kent
002: Glib & Oil by Dominic Leonard
003: Office Poems by Sarah Fletcher
004: Bitter Honey by J H Prynne
005: Belladonna by Suna Afshan
006: Colouring Book by Wayne Holloway-Smith
006.1: Comic Book by Margot Holloway-Smith & Wayne Holloway-Smith
007: _Voss_ by Imogen Cassels
008: Pictures of my Youth by Richard O'Brien
009a/009b: Heredity/Astynome by Naush Sabah
010: Each Sharper Complication by Kyle Lovell

Season 2:
011: Two Odes by Dom Hale
012: I can't promise you anything but whale / fall for you by Jenna Clake
013: Crescent Earth by Astra Papachristodoulou
014: haemorrhage by Aaron Kent
015: Pale Mnemonic by Stuart McPherson
016: Supercutscene by Rishi Dastidar
017: Polychromatics by Maria Sledmere
018: St by Mary Anne Clark
019: Kayfabe by Colin Bancroft
020: One Last Spin Around the Sun by Eva Griffin

SEASON 3:

021: A Tongue Too Long by Taran Spalding-Jenkin
022: Total Furnishing Unit by Charlotte Geater
023: Headspace by Nóra Blascsók
024: The Tricolore Textbook by Wendy Allen
025: Goat Noise by Jasmine Chatfield
026: Bagua by Pey Oh
027: Point Sublime by E. J. Coates
028: Late Morning by Dan Power
029: The Prize by Lucia Dove
030: Council can Kiss my Pitbull by Stevie Kilgour

SEASON 4:

031: Vending Machine by Alex Mazey
032: Lyrical Ballads by Jack Solloway
033: 9 Lives of Jeff Bezos by Rowan Lyster
034: Five Songs on a Cruel Instrument by A. E. Pious (ed. Tristram Fane Saunders)
035: Ordinary Warp by Alex MacDonald
036: Fee Fi Fo Fum by Kym Deyn
037: The Wark Lings Sind by U. G. Világos

LAY OUT YOUR UNREST